Quiknotes

English Bible
Versions

Here are some other useful books
in the *Quiknotes* series.
Add them to your library of
quick-reference books, today:

Quiknotes: The Books of the Bible
Quiknotes: The Books of the New Testament
Quiknotes: The Books of the Old Testament
Quiknotes: The Origin of the Bible
Quiknotes: Christian Classics

ENGLISH BIBLE VERSIONS

Philip W. Comfort, Ph.D.

Tyndale House Publishers, Inc.
WHEATON, ILLINOIS

Library of Congress Cataloging-in-Publication Data

Comfort, Philip Wesley.
  English Bible versions / Philip Wesley Comfort.
    p. cm. — (Quiknotes)
  Includes bibliographical references.
  ISBN 0-8423-3554-4 (softcover : alk. paper)
    1. Bible. English—Versions. 2. Bible. English—Versions—History. I. Title.
II. Quiknotes (Wheaton, Ill.)
BS455.C68 2000
220.5′2—dc21
                                                        99-051621

Printed in the United States of America

06 05 04 03 02 01 00
8   7   6   5   4   3   2   1

CONTENTS

Introduction

NO OTHER BOOK in English history has been more popular than the Bible. Not Shakespeare's plays. Not Hemingway's novels. Not Robert Frost's poetry. The Bible is a perennial best-seller, and it has left an incalculable impact on the cultures of the English-speaking world.

Quik Notes will take us on a journey through the history of the English Bible. We will begin our journey around the time of the earliest versions in the seventh century and travel to the King James Version of 1611, from the King James Version to the Revised Standard Version to the multitude of modern translations published in the last fifty years.

With so many translations of the English Bible now available, people want to know *why* there are so many and what the differences are among them. People also want to know which Bible is best for them. So we will also examine each of the major translations available, noting its strengths, its weaknesses, and the primary purpose for which it was produced. (Each of these translations is also highlighted in the historical overview.) We will consider which Bible translations are best for "pleasure reading" and which are best for careful study. We will learn who the target audience was for each translation—children, adults, Protestants, Catholics, scholars, laypeople.

Through all of this, we can also learn to appreciate the wonderful diversity and availability of God's Word in the English-speaking world.

Philip Comfort, Ph.D.

What's a "Version"?

Before we get into a discussion of various translations of the English Bible, it is important to understand what a Bible version, or translation, is.

Since the Bible is regarded by Christians as God's holy and inspired Word, readers want to be sure that they understand what it truly means as they read. But the Bible was orginally written in Hebrew, Aramaic (a sister language to Hebrew), and Greek. It would be wonderful if everyone could read and understand the Bible in these original languages, but this is not the case. So the Bible has been translated into many of the various languages of the world, including English. In other words, the message of the original languages has been rendered in an understandable way in another language.

As anyone who has learned to speak two different languages has learned, however, there is no single way to translate something from one language into another. There are many different shades of meaning that can be communicated in all sorts of ways. Some shades of meaning can be lost or obscured by certain translation methods, while other methods make them more clear. Many considerations and decisions must be made when making a translation; inevitably, some things will be lost in the process, and others gained.

If we look at Bible translation in the simplest of terms, there are two basic methods. The first is called *formal equivalence* (or word-for-word); the second is called *functional equivalence* (or thought-for-thought). In doing a formal-equivalent translation, the translator attempts to retain as much of the specific wording of the original languages (Hebrew or Greek) as possible when rendering a sentence into the language he or she is working with (in our case, English). In doing a functional-equivalent translation, the translator tries to convey the thoughts of the original languages into the closest natural equivalent in English. This approach places a greater emphasis upon meaning and style than a word-for-word approach does when rendering a sentence in English. The goal of this kind of translation is for a passage to have the same impact upon today's English readers that the original had upon its audience.

The truth of the matter is that not one English translation is either completely word-for-word or completely thought-for-thought. Translations are usually a mixture, with tendencies toward one method or the other.

Most of the older English translations tended to be literal (word-for-word) translations of the original languages. Some modern translations have continued this trend toward literalness. Some of these translators have preferred the literal approach to guard against misrepresenting the text in an attempt to make it more clear. This is a constant danger of thought-for-thought translations, because the more freedom a translator is given in rendering a phrase, the more subjective the process becomes. The thought-for-thought translator must try, in a sense, to enter into the mind of the author. And who can always know with certainty what the author's original intended meaning was? For this reason, a thought-for-thought transla-

DEGREES OF LITERALNESS
A Comparison of the Major Translations

Strictly Literal	*New American Standard Bible*
Literal	King James Version New King James Version Revised Standard Version *The New American Bible*
Literal with Freedom to Be Idiomatic	New Revised Standard Version *The Revised English Bible*
Thought-for-Thought	New International Version *The New Jerusalem Bible* *The New English Bible*
Dynamic Equivalent	Today's English Version New Living Translation Contemporary English Version
Paraphrase	*The Living Bible* *The Message*

tion is usually done with the cooperation of a large group of Bible scholars.

It should be said that the fact that a word-for-word rendering can be executed more consistently than a thought-for-thought one does not make it inherently better. There are also disadvantages to literal translations, especially with respect to readability. Often sentences are rendered in a way that is simply not natural for an English reader, because the translator is reflecting Hebrew or Greek word order and not English. Another casualty from this method is that much of the emotive quality of the original text is lost in translation. In short, literal translations make great study Bibles (because of their consistency of wording) but poor reading Bibles (because of their lack of readability and emotive quality). Because of this, an increasing number of translators in this century have turned to the thought-for-thought approach in an attempt to produce translations that are both reliable and readable—that is, they reliably convey the meaning of the text without sacrificing its readability.

On the previous page is a chart that shows where each of the major translations in use today falls along the spectrum of literalness vs. functional (or "dynamic") equivalence. For more detailed information regarding each of these translations, see "Bible Version Summaries."

Historical Overview

The First Translations into English

The long and fascinating history of the English Bible begins as early as the seventh century. Christianity had spread to London, England, by the third century, and it is possible that the Bible was translated into the native language of the people there, but we have no record of this. We do know that missionaries from Rome brought the Latin Vulgate Bible (the official translation of the Roman Church) to England as early as the fifth century. Christians living in England at that time depended on monks for any kind of instruction from the Bible, and these monks read and taught the Latin Vulgate. After a few centuries, more monasteries were founded, and the need arose for translations of the Bible in English. The earliest English translation, as far as we know, was one done by a seventh-century monk named **Caedmon,** who made a metrical version of parts of the Old and New Testaments. Another English churchman named **Bede** is said to have translated the Gospels into English. Tradition has it that he was translating the Gospel of John on his deathbed in 735. King **Alfred the Great,** a very literate king who reigned from

871–899, included in his laws parts of the Ten Commandments translated into English, and he also translated the Psalms.

The most famous Bible from this period is the **Lindisfarne Gospels** (c. 950). This work contains alternating lines of Latin text and Anglo-Saxon translation.

In the late tenth century, **Aelfric** (c. 955–1020), abbot of Eynsham, made idiomatic translations of various parts of the Bible. Two of these translations still exist. Later, in the 1300s, **William of Shoreham** translated the Psalms into English, as did **Richard Rolle,** whose editions of the Psalms included verse-by-verse commentary. Both of these translations were metrical (and therefore called Psalters) and were popular when John Wycliffe was a young man.

John Wycliffe (c. 1329–1384), the most eminent Oxford theologian of his day, and his associates were the first to translate the entire Bible from Latin into English. Wycliffe's motivation to translate the Bible stemmed partly from his theological battles with the pope. Wycliffe believed that the pope's decrees had to be grounded in Scripture; otherwise they held no authority. This emphasis on the importance of comparing church teaching against the Scriptures led to the need for an understandable translation of the Bible. Wycliffe and his associates completed the New Testament around 1380 and the Old Testament in 1382.

The Reformation

In truth, **William Tyndale** (c. 1494–1536) can be called the father of most modern English translations, because (1) he was the first to translate the Bible from the original languages (a practice that has now become standard policy), (2) many standard versions find their roots in his work, and (3) almost all other English translations have at least been influenced by Tyndale's work and by the myriad of translations that he spawned.

Translations of the Bible prior to the work of William Tyndale were done from the Latin text, which was itself a translation of the original Greek and Hebrew texts of the Bible. With the dawn of the Renaissance, however, renewed interest in the classics made the Greek and Hebrew texts available once again. By translating from the original languages, Tyndale helped to improve the accuracy of English Bibles and set a new standard for Bible translation.

The influence of Tyndale's work was also greatly increased by the invention of the printing press a few decades earlier. The printing press enabled Tyndale's work to be *owned* by the layperson as well as understood by him or her.

Tyndale himself was able to complete only the New Testament, although he also translated several Old Testament books. While Tyndale was in prison, an associate of his named **Miles Coverdale** (1488–1569) brought to completion an entire Bible in English—based largely on Tyndale's translation of the New Testament and some Old Testament books.

Tyndale's work (completed by Coverdale) was the opening of the dike. Since then, there has been a virtual flood of English Bible versions. Among the most noteworthy of the Reformation period are **Thomas Matthew's Version: The Great Bible** (1538), the **Geneva Bible** (1550), the **Bishops' Bible** (1568), and the **Douai-Reims Bible** (1582, 1609–1610). These works prepared the way for the **Authorized King James Version** (KJV or AV) of 1611—a translation that has captured the attention of the English-speaking world even to this day.

The King James Version was the product of a group of scholars commissioned by King James I of England. They were instructed to follow the text of the Bishops' Bible while consulting other translations (Tyndale's, the Geneva Bible, etc.) to obtain the most accurate reading.

Once it was completed, the Authorized King James Version

7

became the standard version of England and the English-speaking world for many centuries, and its resulting influence upon the English language and culture is incalculable. Many individuals tried to improve upon the KJV during the next few centuries, including **John Wesley** (1754), **John Darby** (1871), and **J. B. Rotherham** (1872), but the first consolidated revision did not take place until the latter part of the nineteenth century.

The Nineteenth and Twentieth Centuries

As was mentioned above, the King James Version of the Bible was accepted virtually as the undisputed authority from the time of its release until the end of the nineteenth century. By that time, however, the English language had changed considerably, and several ancient manuscripts of the Bible had been found, whose texts differed slightly from that of the King James Version. These mounting changes spurred a sudden explosion of translations, all of which sought to update the language and text.

The first committee revision of the KJV is known as the **English Revised Version** (1881); the American counterpart to this is the **American Standard Version** (1901). The English Revised Version has passed through two further revisions: the *New English Bible* (1970) and the *Revised English Bible* (1989). The American Standard Version has undergone two separate revisions: the **Revised Standard Version** (1952) and the *New American Standard Bible* (1971). Finally, the Revised Standard Version was further updated to become the **New Revised Standard Version** (1990).

In addition to these standard versions, a multitude of other English translations has appeared in the last two centuries. Many of these have made a significant contribution to the spreading of the Gospel and biblical knowledge. Among the more noteworthy are the following: the *New American Bible* (1970), *The Living*

WILLIAM TYNDALE'S LEGACY
A Family Tree of Translations

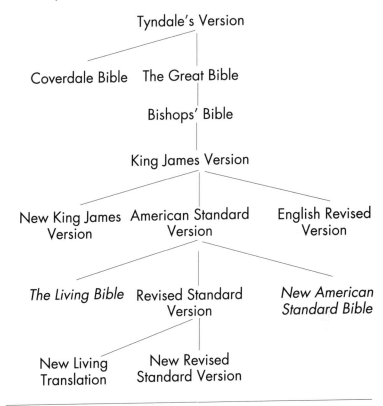

Tyndale's Version

Coverdale Bible   The Great Bible

Bishops' Bible

King James Version

New King James Version   American Standard Version   English Revised Version

The Living Bible   Revised Standard Version   New American Standard Bible

New Living Translation   New Revised Standard Version

Bible (1971), the *Good News Bible:* **Today's English Version** (1966, 1976), the **New International Version** (1978), the *Jerusalem Bible* (1966), the *New Jerusalem Bible* (1986), and the **New Living Translation** (1996).

All of the above-mentioned versions are discussed in more detail in the following pages. They are presented in chronological order. An index at the back of the book gives a full alphabetical listing with corresponding page numbers.

Bible Version Summaries

SECTION ONE
The First Translations into English

Caedmon's Version, c. 675
Caedmon (died c. 678) is the earliest known Christian Anglo-Saxon poet. Our knowledge of him is gained from *Ecclesiastical History* by Bede, an early English historian. Caedmon was an illiterate herdsman who received a vision in which he was commanded to write verse. In this vision he recited verses he had never heard. To his surprise he found that on the next day he could repeat these verses and even add others. His employer, upon hearing of this, introduced him to Hilda, the local abbess of Whitby, who tested his gift by reading aloud a portion of the

Bible, which he was then asked to put into verse. He did so by the following morning. As a result, he was employed in the abbey. He continued until his death to put biblical stories and events of the life of Christ into poetry.

Of all his poetry, "Caedmon's Hymn" is all that survives. It is written in a four-stressed alliterative meter and is similar in style to other Anglo-Saxon poetry. Bede indicated that Caedmon produced a metrical version of parts of the Old and New Testaments. Unfortunately, none of this still exists.

Bede's Version, c. 735

Bede is known as the father of English history and was one of the earliest English Bible translators. Born in what is now Durham and was then the Anglo-Saxon kingdom of Northumbria, Bede entered the monastery at Warmouth when he was seven years old. Soon afterward the whole community moved to Jarrow, where Bede spent the rest of his life, becoming one of the most learned men of Europe. As a youth he devoted himself to the study of Scripture, learning Hebrew, Greek, and Latin. After his ordination he taught in the monastery. Bede used his scholarship to write expositions on Scripture, which were highly prized both in and after his time. In his writings on Mark, Luke, Acts, and Revelation, Bede made use of commentaries by notable church fathers Augustine, Ambrose, Jerome, and Gregory. Bede is said to have translated the Gospels from Latin into English. Tradition has it that he was translating the Gospel of John on his deathbed in 735. Unfortunately, none of his translations have survived.

Alfred the Great's Translations, c. 890

Alfred the Great (reigned 871–899) was considered a very literate king, who revived biblical scholarship in England. He congregated scholars and encouraged learning by setting up a school in which the sons of noblemen were trained. He himself learned how to translate the writings of the significant Christian thinkers into the language of the common person. He included in his laws parts of the Ten Commandments translated into English, and he also translated the Psalms. As far as we know, none of his biblical translations have survived.

Lindisfarne Gospels, c. 950
The Lindisfarne Gospels, also known as the *Book of Durham* or *The Gospels of St. Cuthbert,* are the most famous among the English Bible translations from these early years. This work was produced by the monastery on the island of Lindisfarne, England. It contains the text of the Latin Vulgate with an Anglo-Saxon translation written interlinearly.

Aelfric's Translations, c. 1000
In the late tenth century, Aelfric (c. 955–1020), abbot of Eynsham, was considered the greatest prose writer of his time. He wrote a number of homilies in Anglo-Saxon for the benefit of the rural clergy, and he made idiomatic translations of various parts of the Bible. Two of these translations still exist.

Shoreham's Psalms, Rolle's Psalms, 1300s
In the 1300s, William of Shoreham wrote several religious poems and translated a metrical version of the Psalms from Latin into English. His translation is the earliest complete English Psalter in existence. Richard Rolle also produced a metrical version of the Psalms, which included a verse-by-verse commentary as well. Both of these translations were popular when John Wycliffe was a young man.

Wycliffe's Version, 1380–1382
John Wycliffe (c. 1329–1384), the most eminent Oxford theologian of his day, and his associates were the first to translate the entire Bible from Latin into English. Wycliffe's motivation to translate the Bible stemmed partly from his theological battles with the pope.

Wycliffe has been called the "Morning Star of the Reformation" because he boldly questioned papal authority, criticized the sale of indulgences (which were supposed to release a person from punishment in purgatory), denied the reality of transubstantiation (the doctrine that the bread and wine are changed into Jesus Christ's body and blood during Communion), and spoke out against church hierarchies. The pope reproved Wycliffe for his heretical teachings and asked that Oxford University dismiss him. But Oxford and many government leaders stood with Wycliffe, so he was able to survive the pope's assaults.

Wycliffe's battles with the pope and his belief that the Bible holds an authority above any church teaching or decree help us understand why he would organize a translation of the Bible into the language of the people. Then they could read for themselves what the Scriptures said and see if the church's teachings squared with them. Wycliffe, with his associates, translated from the Latin text and completed the New Testament around 1380 and the Old Testament in 1382. Wycliffe concentrated his labors on the New Testament, while an associate, Nicholas of Hereford, did a major part of the Old Testament.

One of Wycliffe's close associates, John Purvey (c. 1353–1428), continued Wycliffe's work by producing a revision of his translation in 1388. Purvey was an excellent scholar; his work was very well received by his generation and by following generations. Within less than a century, Purvey's revision had replaced the original Wycliffe Bible.

SECTION TWO
Translations during the Reformation

Tyndale's Version
Coverdale's Version
Thomas Matthew's Version: The Great Bible

The Geneva Bible
The Bishops' Bible
Douai-Reims Bible
The Authorized King James Version

Tyndale's Version, 1525
William Tyndale was born in the age of the Renaissance. He graduated in 1515 from Oxford, where he had studied the Scriptures in Greek and in Hebrew—the languages in which they were originally written. By the time he was thirty, Tyndale had committed his life to translating the Bible into English from the Greek and Hebrew texts (which had been made available once again). Tyndale's heart's desire is exemplified in a statement he made to a clergyman when refuting the view that only the clergy were qualified to read and correctly interpret the Scriptures: "If God spare my life, ere many years, I will cause a boy that driveth the plough to know more of the Scripture than thou dost."

In 1523, one year after Martin Luther completed his New Testament in German, Tyndale went to London, seeking a place to work on his English translation. When the bishop of London would not give him hospitality, Humphrey Monmouth, a cloth merchant, provided a place for him. A year later, Tyndale left England for Germany because the English church, which was still under the papal authority of Rome, strongly opposed putting the Bible into the hands of the laity. There in Hamburg, Germany, Tyndale completed the New Testament in English around 1525.

Fifteen thousand copies in six editions were smuggled into England between the years of 1525 and 1530. Church authorities did their best to confiscate copies of Tyndale's translation and burn them, but they couldn't stop the flow of Bibles from Germany into England. Thanks to the newly invented printing press, many copies were available.

Tyndale himself could not return to England because his life was in danger since his translation had been banned. However, he continued to work abroad—correcting, revising, and reissuing his translation until his final revision appeared in 1535. Shortly thereafter, in May of 1535, Tyndale was arrested and carried off to a castle near Brussels. After being in prison for over a year, he was tried and condemned to death. He was strangled and burnt at the stake on October 6, 1536. His final words were so very poignant: "Lord, open the king of England's eyes."

Tyndale had begun work on a translation of the Hebrew Old Testament, but he did not live long enough to complete his task. He had, however, translated the first five books of the Old Testament, Jonah, and some historical books. While Tyndale was in prison, an associate of his named Miles Coverdale (1488–1569) brought to completion an entire Bible in English—based largely on Tyndale's translation of the New Testament and some Old Testament books.

Tyndale can be called the father of most modern English translations because (1) he was the first to translate the Bible from the original languages in which it was written (a practice that has now become standard policy), (2) many standard versions find their roots in his work, and (3) almost all other English translations have at least been influenced by Tyndale's work and by the myriad of translations that he spawned.

Coverdale's Version, 1537

Miles Coverdale was a Cambridge graduate who, like Tyndale, was forced to flee England because he had been strongly influenced by Luther to the extent that he was boldly preaching against Roman Catholic doctrine. While he was abroad, Coverdale met Tyndale and then served as his assistant—especially helping Tyndale translate the first five books of the Old Testament. By the time Coverdale produced a complete translation (1537), the king of England, Henry VIII, had broken all ties with the pope and was ready to see the appearance of an English Bible. Perhaps Tyndale's prayer had been answered—with a very ironic twist. The king gave his royal approval to Coverdale's translation, which was based on the work done by Tyndale, the man Henry VIII had earlier condemned.

Thomas Matthew's Version: The Great Bible, 1537
In the same year that Coverdale's Bible was endorsed by the king (1537), another Bible was published in England. This was the work of Thomas Matthew, a pseudonym for John Rogers (c. 1500–1555), a friend of Tyndale. Evidently, Rogers used Tyndale's unpublished translation of the Old Testament historical books, other parts of Tyndale's translation, and still other parts of Coverdale's translation, to form an entire Bible. This Bible also received the king's approval. Matthew's Bible was revised in 1538 and printed for distribution in the churches throughout England. This Bible, called the Great Bible because of its size and costliness, became the first English Bible authorized for public use.

Many editions of the Great Bible were printed in the early 1540s. However, its distribution was limited. King Henry's attitude toward the new translation changed. As a result, the English Parliament passed a law in 1543 restricting the use of any English translation. It became a crime for any unlicensed person to read or explain the Scriptures in public. Many copies of Tyndale's New Testament and Coverdale's Bible were burned in London.

Greater repression was to follow. After a short period of leniency (during the reign of Edward VI, 1547–1553), severe persecution came from the hands of Mary I (1516–1558). She was a Roman Catholic who was determined to restore Catholicism to England and repress Protestantism. Many Protestants were executed, including John Rogers, the Bible translator. Coverdale was arrested, then released. He fled to Geneva, a sanctuary for English Protestants.

The Geneva Bible, 1550

Protestant English exiles in Geneva chose William Whittingham (c. 1524–1579) to make an English translation of the New Testament for them. He used Theodore Beza's Latin translation and consulted the Greek text. This Bible became very popular because it was small and moderately priced. The preface to the Bible and its many annotations were affected by a strong evangelical influence as well as by the teachings of John Calvin. Calvin was one of the greatest thinkers of the Reformation, a renowned biblical commentator, and the principal leader in Geneva during those days.

The Geneva Bible was very popular with the Puritans and Pilgrims, who brought it with them to America on the *Mayflower* in 1620.

The Bishops' Bible, 1568

While the Geneva Bible was popular among many English men and women, it was not acceptable among many leaders in the Church of England because of its Calvinistic notes. These leaders, recognizing that the Great Bible was inferior to the Geneva Bible in style and scholarship, initiated a revision of the Great Bible. This revised Bible, published in 1568, became known as the Bishops' Bible; it continued in use until it was superseded by the King James Version of 1611.

Douai-Reims Bible, 1582, 1609–1610

This was an English translation of the Latin Vulgate Bible, done by Roman Catholic scholars who were exiled from England. They did their work in the English College at Douai (in the Spanish Netherlands, now part of France). In 1578 the college moved to Rheims, where the New Testament was published in 1582. The Old Testament was completed nearly thirty years later and was published in Douai in 1609–1610.

The men behind this version were Oxford scholars, led by Gregory Martin, William Cardinal Allen, and Thomas Worthington. They did the translation to provide English-speaking Catholics with a Roman Catholic version, thereby giving them an alternative translation to the many Protestant versions being published. Since the Protestant versions often contained notes that were anti-Catholic, this Bible had many notes that were anti-Protestant. Several revisions were made between the years 1749–1772 by Bishop Challoner. Revisions and new editions of the Douai-Reims Bible continued well into the twentieth century.

The Authorized King James Version—AV *or* KJV, *1611*
After James VI of Scotland became the king of England (known as James I), he invited several clergymen from Puritan and Anglican factions to meet together with the hope that differences could be reconciled. The meeting did not achieve this. However, during the meeting one of the Puritan leaders, John Reynolds, president of Corpus Christi College, Oxford, asked the king to authorize a new translation that was more accurate than previous translations. King James liked this idea because the Bishops' Bible had not been successful and because he considered the notes in the Geneva Bible to be seditious. The king initiated the work and took an active part in planning the new translation. He suggested that university professors work on the translation to assure the best scholarship, and he strongly urged that they should not have any marginal notes besides those pertaining to literal renderings from the Hebrew and Greek. The absence of interpretive notes would help the translation be accepted by all the churches in England.

More than fifty scholars, trained in Hebrew and Greek, began the work in 1607. The translation went through several committees before it was finalized. The scholars were instructed to follow the Bishops' Bible as the basic version, as long as it adhered to the original text, and to consult the translations of Tyndale, Matthew, and Coverdale as well as the Great Bible and the Geneva Bible when they appeared to contain more accurate renderings of the original languages. This dependence on other versions is expressed in the preface to the King James Version: "Truly, good Christian reader, we never thought from the beginning that we should need to make a new translation, nor yet to make of a bad one a good one . . . but to make a good one better, or out of many good ones one principal good one."

The King James Version, known in England as the Authorized Version because it was authorized by the king, captured the best of all the preceding English translations and far exceeded all of them. It was the culmination of all the previous English Bible translations; it united high scholarship with Christian devotion and piety. It came into being at a time when the English language was vigorous and beautiful—the age of Elizabethan/Shakespearean English. This version has justifiably been called "the noblest monument of English prose." Indeed, the King James Version has become an enduring monument of English prose because of its gracious style, majestic language, and poetic rhythms. No other book has had such a tremendous influence on English literature, and no other translation has touched the lives of so many English-speaking people for centuries upon centuries, even up to the present day.

SECTION THREE
Translations of the Eighteenth and Nineteenth Centuries
. . . .

Wesley's New Testament
Darby's *New Translation*
Rotherham's *The Emphasized Bible*
English Revised Version
American Standard Version

Wesley's New Testament, 1754

John Wesley (1703–1791) was the leading English evangelist of the eighteenth century and cofounder (with his brother Charles) of Methodism. Along with his well-known accomplishments as a preacher, Wesley was a prolific writer. His "desire to furnish poor people with cheaper, shorter, and plainer books" caused Wesley to write many educational treatises; translations from Greek, Latin, and Hebrew; histories of Rome and England; an ecclesiastical history; and biblical commentaries. He edited *Imitation of Christ* by Thomas à Kempis and works by John Bunyan, Richard Baxter, Jonathan Edwards, Samuel Rutherford, and William Law; he compiled an English dictionary; published twenty-three collections of hymns; and recorded his activities, travels, and spiritual life in his *Journal* (1735–1790). In addition to these writings, Wesley translated Bengel's Greek New Testament *(Gnomon Novi Testamenti)* into English, accompanied by a plethora of textual notes. Wesley's work is called *Explanatory Notes upon the New Testament* (1754).

Darby's New Translation, 1871

John Nelson Darby (1800–1882) is known for being the founder of the Plymouth Brethren and the promoter of a biblical theology known as dispensationalism. Darby left a legacy of scholarly and devotional works. His *Synopsis of the Bible*, thirty-four volumes of *The Collected Works* of J. N. Darby, and three volumes of letters represent his theological views and personal labors. He wrote spiritually rich hymns and poems that displayed his deep affection for Christ. Furthermore, he translated the Bible from the original languages into English, French, and German. The English version, known as the *New Translation*, is still used by members of various Brethren assemblies.

Rotherham's The Emphasized Bible, 1872

In 1872 J. B. Rotherham published a translation of Tregelles's Greek New Testament text, in which he attempted to reflect in English the emphasis inherent in the word order of the Greek text. This translation is still being published under the title *The Emphasized Bible*.

English Revised Version—ERV or RV, 1881

By the latter part of the nineteenth century, the Christian community had been given three very good Greek New Testament texts done by Tregelles, Tischendorf, and Westcott and Hort. These texts were very different from the Textus Receptus, a Greek text that is almost the same as the one used by the translators of the King James Version. Also, more knowledge had been gained about the meaning of various Hebrew and Greek words. Therefore, there was a great need for a new English translation based upon a better text—and with more accurate renderings of the original languages.

The first major corporate effort was initiated in 1870 by the Convocation of Canterbury, which decided to sponsor a major revision of the King James Version. Sixty-five British scholars, working in various committees, made significant changes to the King James Version. The Old Testament scholars corrected mistranslations of Hebrew words and reformatted poetic passages into poetic form. The New Testament scholars made thousands of changes based upon better textual evidence. When the complete Revised Version appeared in 1885, it was received with great enthusiasm. Over 3 million copies sold in the first year of its publication (1881). Its popularity was not long lasting, however, because most people still preferred the King James Version over all other translations.

American Standard Version—ASV, 1885–1901

Several American scholars had been invited to join the revision work on the English Revised Version (1885), with the understanding that any of their suggestions not accepted by the British scholars would appear in an appendix. The American scholars had to agree not to publish their own American revision for fourteen years. When the time came (1901), the American Standard Version was published by several surviving members of the original American committee. This translation, generally regarded as superior to the English Revised Version, is an accurate, literal rendering of very trustworthy texts of both the Old and the New Testaments.

SECTION FOUR
Translations of the First Half of the Twentieth Century
. . . .

The Twentieth Century New Testament
The New Testament in Modern Speech
The New Testament: A New Translation
The Holy Scriptures according to the Masoretic Text
The Complete Bible: An American Translation
The Holy Bible: A Catholic Version by R. Knox
Revised Standard Version

The Twentieth Century New Testament, 1902
The first of the new, free-speech translations was *The Twentieth Century New Testament*. The preface to a new edition of this translation provides an excellent description of the work:

> *The Twentieth Century New Testament* is a smooth-flowing, accurate, easy-to-read translation that captivates its readers from start to finish. Born out of a desire to make the Bible readable and understandable, it is the product of the labors of a committee of twenty men and women who worked together over many years to construct, we believe under divine surveillance, this beautifully simple rendition of the Word of God. (Preface to the new edition [1961] published by Moody Press)

The New Testament in Modern Speech, 1903
A year after the publication of *The Twentieth Century New Testament,* Richard Weymouth published *The New Testament in Modern Speech* (1903). Weymouth, who had received the first Doctor of Literature degree from the University of London, was headmaster of a private school in London. During his life, he produced an edition of the Greek text (*The Resultant Greek Testament,* published in 1862) that was more accurate than the Textus Receptus, and then he labored to produce an English translation of this Greek text in a modern speech version. His translation was very well received; it has gone through several editions and many printings.

The New Testament: A New Translation, 1913
Another new and fresh translation to appear in the early years of this century was one written by James Moffatt, a brilliant Scottish scholar. In 1913 he published his first edition of *The New Testament: A New Translation.* This was actually his second translation of the New Testament; his first was done in 1901 and was called *The Historical New Testament.* In his *New Translation* Moffatt's goal was "to translate the New Testament exactly as one would render any piece of contemporary Hellenistic prose." His work displays brilliance and marked independence from other versions. Unfortunately it was based on Hermann von Soden's Greek New Testament, which reflects a Greek text that was probably less accurate than the other Greek texts available at the time.

The Holy Scriptures according to the Masoretic Text, 1917
The Jewish Publication Society created a translation of the Hebrew Scriptures called *The Holy Scriptures according to the Masoretic Text, A New Translation* (published in 1917). The preface to this translation explains its purpose:

It aims to combine the spirit of Jewish tradition with the results of biblical scholarship, ancient, medieval and modern. It gives to the Jewish world a translation of the Scriptures done by men imbued with the Jewish consciousness, while the non-Jewish world, it is hoped, will welcome a translation that presents many passages from the Jewish traditional point of view.

The Complete Bible: An American Translation, 1923 and 1935
The earliest American modern speech translation was produced by Edgar J. Goodspeed, a professor of New Testament at the University of Chicago. He had criticized *The Twentieth Century New Testament,* Weymouth's version, and Moffatt's translation. Consequently, he was challenged by some other scholars to do better. He took up the challenge and in 1923 published *The New Testament: An American Translation.* When he made this translation, he said that he wanted to give his "version something of the force and freshness that reside in the original Greek." He said, "I wanted my translation to make on the reader something of the impression the New Testament must have made on its earliest readers, and to invite the continuous reading of the whole book at a time." His translation was a success. An Old Testament translation followed in 1935, produced by J. M. Powis Smith and three other scholars.

The Holy Bible: A Catholic Version by R. Knox, 1944 and 1950
In 1943 Pope Pius XII issued the famous encyclical encouraging Roman Catholics to read and study the Scriptures. At the same time, the pope recommended that the Scriptures be translated from the original languages. Previously, all Catholic translations were based on the Latin Vulgate.

Rolland Knox was encouraged by bishops in England to make a fresh translation of the Scriptures, still based on the Latin Vulgate but revised in light of the Hebrew and Greek originals. Knox had converted from Anglicanism to the Roman Catholic church and was ordained a priest in 1917. He taught at St. Edmund's College, Ware, before becoming the chaplain to Roman Catholic students at Oxford University in 1926. He remained at Oxford until 1939. Knox then began his longtime ambition: the translation of the Bible into modern English. The New Testament was published in 1944 and the Old Testament in 1950. It was very popular among English-speaking Roman Catholics.

*Revised Standard Version—*RSV, *1946 and 1952*
The English Revised Version and the American Standard Version had gained a reputation of being accurate study texts but very "wooden" in their construction. The translators who worked on these versions attempted to translate words consistently from the original language regardless of their context and sometimes even followed the word order of the Greek. This created translations that did not read well in English, so there was a need for a new revision.

The demand for a revision was strengthened by the fact that several important biblical manuscripts had been discovered in the 1930s and 1940s—namely, the Dead Sea Scrolls for the Old Testament and the Chester Beatty Papyri for the New Testament. It was felt that the fresh evidence displayed in these documents should be reflected in a revision. The organization that held the copyright to the American Standard Version, called the International Council of Religious Education, authorized a new revision in 1937.

The New Testament translators generally followed the seventeenth edition of the Greek text by Eberhard Nestle (1941), while the Old Testament translators followed the Masoretic text. Both groups, however, adopted readings from other ancient sources when they were considered to be more accurate. The revision showed some textual changes in the book of Isaiah due to the

Isaiah scroll and several changes in the Pauline Epistles due to the Chester Beatty Papyrus, P46. There were other significant revisions. The story of the woman caught in adultery (John 7:52–8:11) was not included in the text but in the margin because none of the early manuscripts contain this story, and the ending to Mark (16:9-20) was not included in the text because it is not found in two very early manuscripts, Codex Vaticanus and Codex Sinaiticus.

The New Testament was published in 1946, and the entire Bible with the Old Testament in 1952. The principles of the revision were specified in the preface to the Revised Standard Version:

> The Revised Standard Version is not a new translation in the language of today. It is not a paraphrase which aims at striking idioms. It is a revision which seeks to preserve all that is best in the English Bible as it has been known and used throughout the years.

This revision was well received by many Protestant churches and soon became their "standard" text. The Revised Standard Version was later published with the Apocrypha of the Old Testament (1957), in a Catholic Edition (1965), and in what is called the *Common Bible,* which includes the Old Testament, the New Testament, and the Apocrypha, with international endorsements by Protestants, Greek Orthodox, and Roman Catholics. Evangelical and fundamental Christians, however, did not receive the Revised Standard Version very well—primarily because of one verse, Isaiah 7:14, which reads, "Therefore the Lord himself will give you a sign. Look, the young woman is with child and shall bear a son, and shall name him Immanuel." Evangelicals and fundamentalists contend that the text should read "virgin," not "young woman." As a result, the Revised Standard Version was panned, if not banned, by many evangelical and fundamental Christians.

27

SECTION FIVE
Translations of the Second Half of the Twentieth Century

. . . .

New Jewish Version
The New English Bible
New American Standard Bible
The Living Bible
The Jerusalem Bible
Good News Bible: Today's English Version
The New American Bible
New International Version
New King James Version
The New Jerusalem Bible
The Revised English Bible

New Jewish Version—NJV, *1962 and 1973*

In 1955 the Jewish Publication Society appointed a new committee of seven eminent Jewish scholars to make a new Jewish translation of the Hebrew Scriptures. The translation, called the New Jewish Version, was published in 1962. A second, improved edition was published in 1973. This work is not a revision of *The Holy Scriptures according to the Masoretic Text;* it is a completely new translation in modern English. The translators attempted to produce a version that would convey the same message to people today as the original text did to the ancient world.

The New English Bible—NEB, *1961 and 1970*

In the year that the New Testament of the Revised Standard Version was published (1946), the Church of Scotland proposed to other churches in Great Britain that it was time for a completely new translation of the Bible. Those who initiated this work asked the translators to produce a fresh translation of the original languages in modern idiom; this was not to be a revision of any foregoing translation, nor was it to be a literal translation. C. H. Dodd, who led the translation project, explains the committee's intentions more fully in the preface to the New Testament (published in 1961)

> The older translators, on the whole, considered that fidelity to the original demanded that they should reproduce, as far as possible, characteristic features of the language in which it was written, such as the syntactical order of words, the structure and division of sentences, and even such irregularities of grammar as were indeed natural enough to authors writing in the easy idiom of popular Hellenistic Greek, but less natural when turned into English. The present translators were enjoined to replace Greek constructions and idioms by those of contemporary English.
>
> This meant a different theory and practice of translation, and one which laid a heavier burden on the translators. Fidelity in translation was not to mean keeping the general framework of the original intact while replacing Greek words by English words more or less equivalent. . . . Thus we have not felt obliged (as did the Revisers of 1881) to make an effort to render the same Greek word everywhere by the same English word. We have in this respect returned to the wholesome practice of King James's men, who (as they expressly state in their preface) recognized no such obligation. We have conceived our task to be that of understanding the original as precisely as we could (using all available aids), and then saying again in our own native idiom what we believed the author to be saying in his.

The entire text of *The New English Bible* was published in 1970; it was well received in Great Britain and in the United States (even though its idioms are extremely British) and was especially praised for its good literary style. The translators were very experimental, producing renderings never before printed in an English version and adopting certain readings from various Hebrew and Greek manuscripts never before adopted. As a result, *The New English Bible* was both highly praised for its ingenuity and severely criticized for its liberty.

New American Standard Bible—NASB, *1963 and 1971*
There are two modern translations that are revisions of (or based on) the American Standard Version (1901): the Revised Standard Version (1952) and the *New American Standard Bible* (1971). The Lockman Foundation, a nonprofit Christian corporation committed to evangelism, promoted this revision of the American Standard Version because "the producers of this translation were imbued with the conviction that interest in the American Standard Version (1901) should be renewed and increased" (from the preface). Indeed, the American Standard Version was a monumental work of scholarship and a very accurate translation. However, its popularity was waning, and it was fast disappearing from the scene. Therefore, the Lockman Foundation organized a team of thirty-two scholars to prepare a new revision. These scholars, all committed to the inspiration of Scripture, strove to produce a literal translation of the Bible in the belief that such a translation "brings the contemporary reader as close as possible to the actual wording and grammatical structure of the original writers" (preface).

The Lockman Foundation instructed translators of the *New American Standard Bible* to adhere to the original languages of the Holy Scriptures as closely as possible and at the same time to obtain a fluent and readable style using current English usage. The New Testament was originally supposed to follow the 23rd edition of the Nestle Greek text, but often it follows the Textus Receptus, which, as mentioned earlier, is a Greek text that is very similar to the one used by King James's translators.

After the *New American Standard Bible* was published (1963 for the New Testament and 1971 for the entire Bible), it received a mixed response. Some critics applauded its literal accuracy, while others sharply criticized its language for hardly being contemporary or modern. On the whole, the *New American Standard Bible* became respected as a good study Bible that accurately reflects the wording of the original languages yet is not a good translation for Bible reading.

A revision of the NASB was done in 1996, which primarily involved updating some of the more archaic terms, such as *Thee* and *Thou.*

The Living Bible—TLB, *1966 and 1971*

In 1962 Kenneth Taylor published a paraphrase of the New Testament Epistles in a volume called *Living Letters.* This new dynamic paraphrase, written in common vernacular, was well received and became widely acclaimed—especially for its ability to communicate the message of God's Word to the common person. In the beginning its circulation was greatly enhanced by the endorsement of the Billy Graham Evangelistic Association, which distributed thousands of free copies and did much to publicize the book. Taylor continued to paraphrase other portions of the Bible and publish successive volumes: *Living Prophecies* (1965), *Living Gospels* (1966), *Living Psalms* (1967), *Living Lessons of Life and Love* (1968), *Living Books of Moses* (1969), and *Living History of Moses* (1970). The entire *Living Bible* was published in 1971 (the *Living New Testament* was printed in 1966).

Using the American Standard Version as his working text, Taylor rephrased the Bible into modern speech—such that anyone, even a child, could understand the message of the original writers. In the preface to *The Living Bible* Taylor explains his view of paraphrasing:

To paraphrase is to say something in different words than the author used. It is a restatement of the author's thoughts, using different words than he did. This book is a paraphrase of the Old and New Testaments. Its purpose is to say as exactly as possible what the writers of the Scriptures meant, and to say it simply, expanding where necessary for a clear understanding by the modern reader.

Even though many modern readers have greatly appreciated the fact that *The Living Bible* made God's Word clear to them, Taylor's paraphrase has been criticized for being highly interpretive—a characteristic that is both a strength and a weakness of all paraphrases. Taylor was aware of this danger when he made the paraphrase. Again, the preface clarifies:

There are dangers in paraphrases, as well as values. For whenever the author's exact words are not translated from the original languages, there is a possibility that the translator, however honest, may be giving the English reader something that the original writer did not mean to say.

The Living Bible has been very popular among English readers worldwide. More than 40 million copies have been sold by Tyndale House Publishers, which Taylor specifically created to publish his paraphrase. The name of this company reflects Taylor's ultimate intentions, for it is named after William Tyndale, the father of many modern English translations of the Bible.

The Jerusalem Bible—JB, 1966
The Jerusalem Bible, published in England in 1966, is the English counterpart to a French translation entitled *La Bible de Jerusalem.* The French translation was "the culmination of decades of research and biblical scholarship" (from the preface to

The Jerusalem Bible) and was published by the scholars of the Dominican Biblical School of Jerusalem. This Bible, which includes the Apocrypha, contains many study helps such as introductions to each book of the Bible, extensive notes on various passages, and maps. The study helps are an intricate part of the whole translation because it is the belief of Roman Catholic leadership that laypeople should be given interpretive helps in their reading of the sacred text. The study helps in *The Jerusalem Bible* were translated from the French, whereas the Bible text itself was translated from the original languages with the help of the French translation. The translation of the text produced under the editorship of Alexander Jones is considerably freer than other translations, such as the Revised Standard Version, because the translators sought to capture the meaning of the original writings in a "vigorous, contemporary literary style" (from the preface to *The Jerusalem Bible*).

Good News Bible: Today's English Version—TEV, 1966 and 1976
The New Testament in Today's English Version, also known as *Good News for Modern Man,* was published by the American Bible Society in 1966. The translation was originally done by Robert Bratcher, a research associate of the Translations Department of the American Bible Society, and then further refined by the American Bible Society. The translation, heavily promoted by several Bible societies and very affordable, sold more than 35 million copies within six years of the time of printing. The New Testament translation, based upon the first edition of the *Greek New Testament* (the United Bible Societies, 1966), is rendered in modern, idiomatic, and simple English. The translation was greatly influenced by the linguistic theory of *dynamic equivalence*—a further development of the functional equivalence (thought-for-thought) approach to translation—and was quite successful in providing English readers with a translation that,

for the most part, accurately reflects the meaning of the original texts. This is explained in the preface to the New Testament:

> This translation of the New Testament has been prepared by the American Bible Society for people who speak English as their mother tongue or as an acquired language. As a distinctly new translation, it does not conform to traditional vocabulary or style, but seeks to express the meaning of the Greek text in words and forms accepted as standard by people everywhere who employ English as a means of communication. Today's English Version of the New Testament attempts to follow, in this century, the example set by the authors of the New Testament books, who, for the most part, wrote in the standard, or common, form of the Greek language used throughout the Roman Empire.

Because of the success of the New Testament, the American Bible Society was asked by other Bible societies to make an Old Testament translation following the same principles used in the New Testament. The entire Bible was published in 1976 and is known as the *Good News Bible:* Today's English Version.

*The New American Bible—*NAB, *1970*
The first American Catholic Bible to be translated from the original languages is *The New American Bible* (not to be confused with the *New American Standard Bible*). Although this translation was published in 1970, work had begun on this version several decades before. Prior to Pope Pius's encyclical, an American translation of the New Testament based on the Latin Vulgate was published—known as the Confraternity Version. After the encyclical, the Old Testament was translated from the Hebrew Masoretic text and the New Testament redone, based on the twenty-fifth edition of the Greek Nestle-Aland text. *The New*

American Bible has short introductions to each book of the Bible
and very few marginal notes. Sakae Kubo and Walter Specht
provide a just description of the translation itself:

> The translation itself is simple, clear, and straightforward
> and reads very smoothly. It is good American English, not
> as pungent and colorful as the N.E.B. *[New English Bible]*.
> Its translations are not striking but neither are they clumsy.
> They seem to be more conservative in the sense that they
> tend not to stray from the original. That is not to say that
> this is a literal translation, but it is more faithful. (*So Many
> Versions?*, 165)

New International Version—NIV, 1973 and 1978
The New International Version is a completely new rendering of
the original languages done by an international group of more than
one hundred scholars. These scholars worked many years and in
several committees to produce an excellent thought-for-thought
translation in contemporary English for private and public use. The
New International Version is called "international" because it was
prepared by distinguished scholars from English-speaking countries such as the United States, Canada, Great Britain, Australia,
and New Zealand, and because the translators sought to use vocabulary common to the major English-speaking nations of the world.

The translators of the New International Version sought to
make a version that was midway between a literal rendering (as
in the *New American Standard Bible*) and a free paraphrase (as
in *The Living Bible*). Their goal was to convey in English the
thoughts of the original writers. This is succinctly explained in
the original preface to the New Testament:

> Certain convictions and aims guided the translators. They
> are all committed to the full authority and complete trust-

worthiness of the Scriptures. Therefore, their first concern was the accuracy of the translation and its fidelity to the thought of the New Testament writers. While they weighed the significance of the lexical and grammatical details of the Greek text, they have striven for more than a word-for-word translation. Because thought patterns and syntax differ from language to language, faithful communication of the meaning of the writers of the New Testament demanded frequent modifications in sentence structure and constant regard for the contextual meanings of words.

Concern for clarity of style—that it should be idiomatic without being idiosyncratic, contemporary without being dated—also motivated the translators and their consultants. They have consistently aimed at simplicity of expression, with sensitive attention to the connotation and sound of the chosen word. At the same time, they endeavored to avoid a sameness of style in order to reflect the varied styles and moods of the New Testament writers.

The New Testament of the New International Version was published in 1973, and the entire Bible in 1978. This version has been phenomenally successful. Millions and millions of readers have adopted the New International Version as "their" Bible. Since 1987 it has outsold the King James Version, the best-seller for centuries—a remarkable indication of its popularity and acceptance in the Christian community. The New International Version, sponsored by the New York Bible Society (now the International Bible Society) and published by Zondervan Publishers, has become a standard version used for private reading and pulpit reading in many English-speaking countries.

New King James Version—NKJV, 1982
The New King James Version, published in 1982, is a revision of

the King James Version. As such, the New King James Version follows the historic precedent of the Authorized Version in maintaining a literal approach to translation. The revisers have called this method of translation "complete equivalence." This means that the revisers sought to provide a complete representation of all the information in the original text with respect to the history of usage and etymology of words in their contexts.

The most distinctive feature of the NKJV is its underlying original text. The revisers of the NKJV New Testament chose to use the Textus Receptus—a Greek text very similar to that used by the King James translators—rather than modern critical editions, including the Majority Text and the Nestle-Aland text. By way of concession, they have footnoted any significant textual variation from the Majority Text and modern critical editions. The Majority Text, which is the text supported by the majority of all known New Testament manuscripts, hardly differs from the Textus Receptus; thus, there are few significant differences noted. There are well over a thousand differences footnoted regarding the Nestle-Aland/United Bible Societies' text.

Though exhibiting an antiquated text, the language of the NKJV is modern. All the Elizabethan English of the original King James Version has been replaced with contemporary American English. Though much of the sentence structure of the NKJV is still dated and stilted, contemporary readers who favor the spirit of the King James Version but can't understand much of its archaic language will appreciate this revision.

The New Jerusalem Bible—NJB, *1986*

The Jerusalem Bible had become widely used for liturgical purposes, for study, and for private reading. This success spurred a new revision, both of *La Bible de Jerusalem* in French and *The Jerusalem Bible* in English. This new edition "incorporated progress in scholarship over the two decades since the preparation of the first edition. The introductions and notes were often widely changed to take into account linguistic, archaeological, and theological advances, and the text itself in some instances reflected new understanding of the originals" (from the foreword). *The New Jerusalem Bible* (published in 1986) generally has been received as an excellent study text. The New Testament offers some interesting variations (especially in the book of Acts), where the translators have chosen to follow a Greek text that is different from those most widely accepted as the probable original text.

The Revised English Bible—REB, 1989

The Revised English Bible (1989) is a revision of *The New English Bible* (NEB), which was published in 1971. Because the NEB gained such popularity in British churches and was regularly used for public reading, several British churches decided there should be a revision of the NEB to keep the language current and the text up-to-date with modern biblical scholarship.

For the Old Testament, the revisers used the Masoretic text as it appears in *Biblia Hebraica Stuttgartensia* (1967, 1977). They also made use of the Dead Sea Scrolls and a few other important versions, including the Septuagint. The revisers of the New Testament used Nestle-Aland's *Novum Testamentum Graece* (26th edition, 1979) as their base text. This choice resulted in several textual changes from *The New English Bible* text, which followed a very eclectic text. The Greek text used by the NEB was decided upon by the translation committee on a verse-by-verse basis. The resulting Greek text was very uneven and yet very interesting. The translators of the NEB adopted readings never before put into print by English translators. The scholars working on *The Revised English Bible* eliminated many of these readings, however, in the interest of providing a more balanced text.

SECTION SIX
Translations of the Last Decade
. . . .

New Revised Standard Version
Contemporary English Version
New Century Version
New Life Version
The Message
God's Word
New Living Translation

New Revised Standard Version—NRSV, *1990*
The New Revised Standard Version, published in 1990, is an
excellent example of the current trend to publish revisions rather
than new translations. In the preface to this revision, Bruce
Metzger, chair of the revision committee, wrote:

> The New Revised Standard Version of the Bible is an
> authorized revision of the Revised Standard Version, pub-
> lished in 1952, which was a revision of the American Stan-
> dard Version, published in 1901, which, in turn, embodied
> earlier revisions of the King James Version, published in
> 1611.
>   The need for issuing a revision of the Revised Standard
> Version of the Bible arises from three circumstances:
> (1) the acquisition of still older biblical manuscripts,
> (2) further investigation of linguistic features of the text,
> and (3) changes in preferred English usage.

Metzger's three reasons for producing the New Revised Standard Version are essentially the same reasons behind all revisions of Bible translations.

Of all the translations, the NRSV most closely follows the text
of Nestle-Aland's *Novum Testamentum Graece* (26th edition,

1979). No doubt this is due to Bruce Metzger's involvement in both editorial committees—a leading member of the Nestle-Aland committee and the chair for the NRSV committee.

Perhaps the most notable feature of the NRSV is its attention to gender-inclusive language. While respecting the historicity of the ancient texts, the NRSV translators attempted to make this new revision more palpable to modern readers by avoiding unnecessarily masculine renderings wherever possible. For example, in the New Testament Epistles, the believers are referred to as *adelphoi,* which is traditionally rendered "brothers," yet it is clear that these epistles were addressed to *all* the believers—both male and female. Thus, the NRSV translators have used such phrases as "brothers and sisters" or "friends" (always with a footnote saying "Greek, brothers") in order to represent the historical situtation while remaining sensitive to modern readers.

Metzger and the other translators tried to be careful, however, not to overemphasize the gender-inclusive principle. Some readers had been hoping for a more radical revision regarding gender-inclusiveness, including changing such phrases as "God our Father" to "God our Parent." But the NRSV revisers decided against this approach, considering it an inaccurate reflection of the original text's intended meaning.

Contemporary English Version—CEV, 1991 and 1994
Barclay Newman of the American Bible Society is the pioneer of a new translation for early youth. Working according to Eugene Nida's model of functional equivalence, Newman, in cooperation with other members of the American Bible Society, produced fresh translations of New Testament books based on the United Bible Societies' *Greek New Testament* (third, corrected edition, 1983). These first appeared as individual books: *A Book about Jesus* (containing passages from the four Gospels), *Luke Tells the Good News about Jesus,* and *Good News Travels Fast: The Acts*

of the Apostles. Then the complete New Testament was published in 1991. With the aid of other scholars, Barclay Newman completed the entire Bible in 1994.

The CEV aims to be both reliable to the original languages and readable for modern English speakers. In producing this kind of translation, the translators constantly asked two questions: What do the words mean? and What is the most accurate and natural way to express this meaning in contemporary English? Since many technical terms such as *salvation, grace,* and *righteousness* do not readily communicate to modern readers, the CEV translators have sought natural English equivalents such as "God saves you," "God is kind to you," and "God accepts you." Sometimes translators cannot avoid using difficult terms in the text (such as *Pharisee, Day of Atonement,* and *circumcise*) because these words hold religious significance that cannot easily be conveyed in simpler terms. In order to help the reader with these words, the CEV defines such terms in a separate word list.

New Century Version—NCV, 1991

The New Century Version is a new translation of the original languages published in two editions: one for children, called the *International Children's Bible*; and one for adults, first appearing in a New Testament edition called *The Word* and now available with the entire Bible text in an edition called *The Everyday Bible,* published by Sweet.

The World Bible Translation Center developed the New Century Version by using an existing translation specifically prepared for the deaf, which was unique in that it used a limited vocabulary. The translators then made a new version based on the latest edition of *Biblia Hebraica Stuttgartensia* for the Old Testament and the third edition of the United Bible Societies' *Greek New Testament* for the New Testament. (The translation for the deaf was published as *New Testament for the Deaf,* Baker Book House.)

Both editions of the NCV emphasize simplicity and clarity of expression. The children's edition, however, is stylistically simpler than the adults' edition. The translators of the NCV wanted to make "the language simple enough for children to read and understand for themselves" (preface). Therefore, the translators used short, uncomplicated sentences, as well as vocabulary appropriate for children on a third-grade instructional level.

New Life Version, 1993

The New Life Version, produced by Gleason H. Ledyard, was first published as the *Children's New Testament* (1966). While serving as missionaries in northern Canada, Ledyard and his wife, Kathryn, worked with Eskimos who were just starting to learn English. This experience created a desire within the Ledyards to make an English translation for people learning English as a second language. After translating a few books of the Bible and distributing them to various people, they were told that their translation was excellent for children. Thus, the Ledyards continued their work, finishing first the New Testament and then the Old Testament. This work became the New Life Version, published by Christian Literature International.

The key to this version's readability is that it uses a limited vocabulary and simplifies difficult biblical terms. With more than 6 million copies sold, the New Life Version has been published in many editions and has been distributed worldwide—especially to those who are learning English as a second language. This version is the text of the *Precious Moments Children's Bible,* published by Baker Book House (1993).

The Message, 1994

One of the most recent New Testament translations to come onto the publishing scene is *The Message* by Eugene H. Peterson (published by NavPress). Peterson was inspired to produce his idiomatic English translation because, as he says, he had been doing this throughout his vocational life:

> For thirty-five years as a pastor I stood at the border between two languages, biblical Greek and everyday English, acting as a translator, providing the right phrases, getting the right words so that the men and women to whom I was pastor could find their way around and get along in this world where God has spoken so decisively and clearly in Jesus.

Peterson's goal in creating a translation of the New Testament was to convert the tone, the rhythm, the events, and the ideas of the Greek text into the way we actually think and speak in English. This was quite ambitious. In some places Peterson seems to have accomplished his goal, as in his rendering of Romans 1:25: "They traded the true God for a fake god, and worshiped the god they made instead of the God who made them." But in other places, Peterson seems simply to re-present the Greek text in very awkward English. This is most apparent in the prologue to John's Gospel, where many expressions are often confusing to those unfamiliar with Greek. No doubt many readers will be hard-pressed to follow what Peterson is trying to do in John 1:1: "The Word was first, the Word present to God, God present to the Word." Likewise, in John 1:18 Peterson uses a fairly awkward phrase: "This one-of-a-kind God-Expression, who exists at the very heart of the Father, has made him plain as day."

God's Word, 1995

The biblical translation presently named *God's Word* (1995) has been referred to by several names in the past few years. It has been *God's Word to the Nations: New Evangelical Translation,*

43

and it has been called *New Evangelical Translation* (1988). Modeled after William Beck's version, *An American Translation* (New Testament, 1963; entire Bible, 1976), this translation is the result of the publishing effort of a Lutheran group called God's Word to the Nations Bible Society.

The motivation behind this version was to provide English-reading people throughout the world with an accurate, clear, and easy-to-read translation of the Bible. With this in mind, the revisers avoided heavy theological jargon that may not be meaningful to nontheologically trained readers. Thus, they did not use words like *covenant, grace, justify, repent,* and *righteousness.* Rather, they employed common words to convey the meaning of the original text. The revisers have called this theory of translation "natural equivalence." It is supposed to avoid the extremes of form equivalence (awkwardness due to strict literalness) and function equivalance (inaccuracy due to oversimplification).

New Living Translation—NLT, *1996*
With over 40 million copies in print, *The Living Bible* has been a very popular version of the Bible for more than thirty years. But various criticisms spurred the author of *The Living Bible,* Kenneth Taylor, to revise his paraphrase. Under the sponsorship of Tyndale House Publishers, Taylor's company, *The Living Bible* underwent a thorough revision. More than ninety evangelical scholars from various theological backgrounds and denominations worked for seven years to produce the New Living Translation. As a result, the NLT is more faithful to the original text and yet is still dynamic and easy to understand.

Whereas Ken Taylor used the ASV (1901) as his base text for *The Living Bible,* the scholars carefully revised the text of *The Living Bible* acccording to the latest critical editions of the Hebrew and Greek texts. For the Old Testament, the revisers used the Masoretic text as it appears in *Biblia Hebraica Stutt-*

gartensia (1967, 1977). They also made use of the Dead Sea Scrolls and a few other important versions, including the Septuagint. The revisers of the New Testament used the text of Nestle-Aland's *Novum Testamentum Graece* (27th edition, 1993) as their base text.

The New Living Translation continues Taylor's policy of dynamic, or functional, equivalence, attempting to use the closest natural equivalent of the message of the Hebrew and Greek texts—both in meaning and in style. Such a translation seeks to have the same impact upon modern readers as the original had upon its audience. As we have mentioned earlier, such a method makes the translation vulnerable to the personal beliefs and biases of the translator—a frequent criticism of *The Living Bible*—but Taylor was able to guard against this problem by utilizing such a large group of scholars, each of whom was well studied in his or her particular area. To ensure that the translation would be extremely readable and understandable, a group of stylists adjusted the wording to make it clear and fluent.

The value of a thought-for-thought translation can be illustrated by an example given in the preface to the New Living Translation. First Kings 2:10 in the NIV reads: "Then David rested with his fathers and was buried in the City of David" (NIV). In the NLT, the translators wanted to directly communicate the meaning of the phrase "rested with his fathers" to the modern reader, so they translated the verse as "Then David died and was buried in the City of David" (NLT).

TIMELINE OF
BIBLE VERSIONS
AND RELATED EVENTS

c. 30	Jesus' crucifixion and resurrection
c. 95	New Testament completed (in Greek)
c. 400	Latin Vulgate (Jerome's translation)
c. 600	Christianity takes root in England
c. 650	Caedmon's metrical versions
c. 735	Bede's Gospels
800	Charlemagne is crowned emperor of the Holy Roman Empire
871–899	Alfred the Great's Psalms and Decalogue
950	The Lindisfarne Gospels
955–1020	Aelfric's translations
1066	William of Normandy conquers England
c. 1325	Rolle and Shoreham's metrical Psalms
1380–1382	Wycliffe's translation of the Bible
c. 1450	Johannes Gutenberg invents the printing press
1516	Erasmus's Greek New Testament—the forerunner to the Textus Receptus
1517	Martin Luther nails his Ninety-five Theses to the chapel door
1525	William Tyndale's translation of the New Testament
1534	Henry VIII establishes the Church of England
1537	Coverdale's Version
1538	The Great Bible
1550	The Geneva Bible
1568	The Bishops' Bible
1582, 1609–1610	Douai-Reims Bible
1611	Authorized King James Version
1616	William Shakespeare dies
1620	Pilgrims arrive in America

1754	Wesley's New Testament
1776	The American Revolution
1859	Codex Sinaiticus discovered by Tischendorf
1871	John Darby's *New Translation*
1872	Rotherdam's *Emphasized Bible*
1881	English Revised Version
1890	Photographs of Codex Vaticanus made available
1901	American Standard Version
1902	*The Twentieth Century New Testament*
1903	*The New Testament in Modern Speech*
1913	*The New Testament: A New Translation*
1917	*The Holy Scriptures according to the Masoretic Text*
1918	World War I ends
1923, 1935	Goodspeed's *The Complete Bible: An American Translation*
1944, 1950	*The Holy Bible:* A Catholic Version
1945	World War II ends
1946, 1952	Revised Standard Version
1948	Dead Sea Scrolls discovered
1955	New Jewish Version
1961, 1970	*The New English Bible*
1963, 1971	*New American Standard Bible*
1966, 1971	*The Living Bible*
1966	*The Jerusalem Bible*
1966, 1976	*Good News Bible:* Today's English Version
1970	*The New American Bible*
1973, 1978	New International Version
1982	New King James Version
1986	*The New Jersualem Bible*
1989	*The Revised English Bible*
1990	New Revised Standard Version
1991	Dead Sea Scrolls text made available to the public
1991	New Century Version
1991, 1994	Contemporary English Version
1993	New Life Version
1994	*The Message*
1995	*God's Word*
1996	New Living Translation

ALPHABETICAL
LISTING OF
BIBLE VERSIONS

Aelfric's translations (955–1020)

Alfred the Great's Psalms and Decalogue (871–899)

American Standard Version (1901)

Authorized King James Version (1611)

Bede's Gospels (c. 735)

The Bishops' Bible (1568)

Caedmon's metrical versions (c. 650)

Goodspeed's *The Complete Bible: An American Translation*
  (1923, 1935)

Contemporary English Version (1991, 1994)

Coverdale's Version (1537)

Darby's *New Translation* (1871)

Douai-Reims Bible (1582, 1609–1610)

English Revised Version (1881)

The Geneva Bible (1550)

God's Word (1995)

Good News Bible: Today's English Version (1966, 1976)

The Great Bible (1538)

The Holy Bible: A Catholic Version (1944, 1950)

The Holy Scriptures according to the Masoretic Text (1917)

The Jerusalem Bible (1966)

Latin Vulgate (Jerome's translation) (c. 400)

The Lindisfarne Gospels (950)

The Living Bible (1966, 1971)

The Message (1994)
The New American Bible (1970)
New American Standard Bible (1963, 1970)
New Century Version (1991)
The New English Bible (1961, 1970)
New International Version (1973, 1978)
The New Jerusalem Bible (1986)
New Jewish Version (1955)
New King James Version (1982)
New Life Version (1993)
New Living Translation (1996)
New Revised Standard Version (1990)
The New Testament: A New Translation (1913)
The New Testament in Modern Speech (1903)
New Translation (1871)
The Revised English Bible (1989)
Revised Standard Version (1946, 1952)
Rolle's and Shoreham's metrical Psalms (c. 1325)
Rotherham's *The Emphasized Bible* (1872)
The Twentieth Century New Testament (1902)
Wesley's New Testament (1754)
William Tyndale's translation of the New Testament (1525)
William Tyndale's translation of various Old Testament books (1526–1535)
Wycliffe's translation of the Bible (1380–1382)

FOR FURTHER READING

Bailey, Lloyd R. *The Word of God: A Guide to English Versions of the Bible.* Louisville, Ky.: Westminster John Knox Press, 1982.

Bruce, F. F. *The History of the Bible in English: From the Earliest Versions to Today.* New York: Oxford University Press, 1978.

————. *The Books and the Parchments.* Old Tappan, N.J.: Fleming H. Revell Co., 1984.

The Cambridge History of the Bible. 3 vols. New York: Cambridge University Press, 1975.

Carson, D. A. *The King James Version Debate: A Plea for Realism.* Grand Rapids: Baker Book House, 1979.

Comfort, Philip W., ed. *The Origin of the Bible.* Wheaton, Ill.: Tyndale House Publishers, 1992.

Glassman, Eugene H. *The Translation Debate: What Makes a Translation Good?* Downers Grove, Ill.: InterVarsity Press, 1981.

Kubo, Sakae and Walter Specht. *So Many Versions?* Revised and enlarged ed. Grand Rapids: Zondervan, 1983.

Lewis, Jack P. *The English Bible from KJV to NIV.* Grand Rapids: Baker Book House, 1982.

Long, John D. *The Bible in English: John Wycliffe and William Tyndale.* Lanham, Md.: University Press of America, 1998.

Opfell, Olga S. *King James Bible Translators.* Jefferson, N.C.: McFarland & Co, Inc., 1982.

Sheeley, Steven M. and Robert N. Nash, Jr. *The Bible in English Translation: An Essential Guide.* Nashville: Abingdon Press, 1997.

Vance, Laurence M. *A Brief History of English Bible Translations.* Pensacola, Fla.: Vance Publications, 1993.

White, James R. *The King James Only Controversy: Can You Trust the Modern Translations?* Minneapolis: Bethany House, 1995.